Entering the Stream

Entering the Stream

Poems about Union

N. Thomas Johnson-Medland

RESOURCE *Publications* • Eugene, Oregon

ENTERING THE STREAM
Poems about Union

Copyright © 2011 N. Thomas Johnson-Medland. All rights reserved. Except for brief quotations in critical publications or reviews, no part of this book may be reproduced in any manner without prior written permission from the publisher. Write: Permissions, Wipf and Stock Publishers, 199 W. 8th Ave., Suite 3, Eugene, OR 97401.

Resource Publications
An Imprint of Wipf and Stock Publishers
199 W. 8th Ave., Suite 3
Eugene, OR 97401

www.wipfandstock.com

ISBN 13: 978-1-61097-139-3

Manufactured in the U.S.A.

"Yesterday, in Louisville, at the corner of 4th and Walnut, suddenly realized that I loved all the people and that none of them were, or, could be totally alien to me. As if waking from a dream—the dream of my separateness, of the "special" vocation to be different. My vocation does not really make me different from the rest of men or put me in a special category except artificially, juridically. I am still a member of the human race—and what more glorious destiny is there for man, since the Word was made flesh and became, too, a member of the Human Race!"
—*Thomas Merton*

"I am the light that is over all things. I am all: from me all came forth, and to me all attained. Split a piece of wood; I am there. Lift up the stone, and you will find me there."
—*Jesus*, The Gospel of Thomas, verse 77

"Pilgrimage to the place of the wise is to find escape from the flame of separateness."
—*Jalalu 'ddin Rumi*

> *

Introduction

THE NOTION AND phrase of "entering the stream" has long been an image for merger and union. Most often it is meant to sum up the idea of union with the Divine Principle or God. Less often, yet still common, it is used to image the union of ideas, bodies, and movements.

The sense that one thing folds into or flows into another and gets lost is still a major underpinning toward the belief that there is some "ah ha" moment in life where we are able to drift out of simple, commonplace existence and enter the field of ALL knowing. We believe that there can be and is a moment of merger (a born-again instant) an awakening to something outside of what it means to be singularly dual.

It is not by chance that the two sacramental rites within Christianity that have the deepest roots in the gathered community over time—reaching down into the loam of our existence—are Baptism and Eucharist. The first—the initiation rite—is about dissolving into God and His mercy and forgiveness. We enter into Him and the fullness of His Kingdom. We are overwhelmed by the waters and emerge a new creature. The second—the continuation rite—is about God dissolving into us. He enters us bringing the fullness of His Kingdom. We ingest God (depending upon your theology) in either image or fact and we emerge a new creature.

We are swallowed up by God. We swallow up God.

Both of these rites of the Christian faith are from among the ken of mythological tales told over and over in time immemorial among all of man's quests for meaning and placement in this universe. We somehow wrestle with being consumed by the ALL and we also wrestle with consuming the ALL.

You do not have to look hard to find the stories of Chronos all over the landscape of human growth and development—either in story or psyche. Man gobbles up that which is around him—things that pose a threat and things that do not.

+ + +

Poetry, like prayer, is a ladder in. It takes us into either the heart of the individual (the self) or into the heart of the Divine (the Self). And, although the "in" we refer to in entering into the Self is somewhat of an outward movement "In"—beyond ourselves into the ONE—it is nonetheless a move into the non-local identity we possess in God.

The words of poetry and prayer are vehicles of experience. Poems take us to the experience of the Self/self. Theology, history, biology, cartography, geology and all the other "ologies" and "ographies" take us to the edge of experience, narrating and describing all that is about us—all that we see "out there".

Poetry can take us from the outer edges of simple description into the creative landscape of "Presence", which is of course what distinguishes the boundary between "knowledge about" and "knowledge of". Poetry and prayer are "experiences of", not just "experiences about". They are about the "in here" of the "out there".

Poetry is nothing less than hopping from rock to rock into the experience of "what is" itself. It tends to prepare the heart for exploding out and connecting with what is outside (and inside) in a visceral primal union. All at once.

Rumi was a master of the "in here" and "out there". His poems are able to weld us to the Creative Father—to force us open and into union. You can read his poems and get lost hopping across the river; one stone at a time until you fall in—to the DIVINE PRESENCE—and drown.

Poems tend to get us closer to this mystic heart because they leap across cavernous divides of ideas, emotions, and being. They bring together things that we do not normally see as one. Their leaping builds up a momentum in us that hurls us into a space of conjunction; uniting us with all that there is.

+ + +

Poems smash our left and right hemispheres together and produce little images that we never knew existed. The connected notions that emerge from poems are genuine sacramental rites of initiation and continuation. Poems help us consume and be consumed. This must ultimately remind us that the truly "spiritual life" is the "poetic life". Praying is poetry-making in its most visceral form.

While one image for the poetic process is jumping rock to rock and falling in, another image is the flowing of "all that is the stream" into the "Oneness that is the Ocean". Neurologically it is seen as the (Paul MacLean) developmental flow of brain systems from the reptilian brain, through the limbic system, into the neo-cortex. It is the process of bringing the many into union—connecting: merging all of our ways of BEING in this body. Lower thinking moves into higher thinking and associations are made.

Liturgical forms are poems. Liturgical formulas are how the masters of any spiritual tradition passed on the way of becoming one with the Divine. Liturgy provides the rock-hopping space of poetry. Liturgy gets us into "consuming space"—to eat and be eaten. Liturgy, like poetry puts us "out of our mind". It is a place that religion would do well to visit—the space of eating God and being eaten by God. The union of all opposites is nothing more than an image of consuming and being consumed.

The momentum that builds up in us as we approach union with the One—with the Mystic Father—is clearly a process that we interact with over time. Like Peter in his protestation to Jesus that he was not going to allow the Master to wash his feet, we sometimes start out pushing the idea of union away—as if it is somehow repulsive. As time passes and the experience takes hold in us, we become lost in the delirium of the connection. We echo Peter's intent that we do not just want our feet washed, but every inch of us—all of us. We become intoxicated by and with the experience and want to be consumed and to consume all at once; all of the time.

+ + +

The experiences of romantic love and of death mirror this passionate consummation process. In both, we are overwhelmed—taken-over by a larger than life pathos/ethos that emerges from God-knows-where. Perhaps the bliss and grief mechanisms in our lives are more the same than we would be willing to admit. Perhaps "Penthos" and "Ecstasis" are twin singularities. However this is organized in the life of the universal and the individual, both passion and grief tend to work themselves into these poems. Both require abandonment and surrender.

The perpetual ebb and flow of the life of earth-seasons and human growth and development are signposts pointing to the ever changing surface of the Oneness below all life and consciousness. What we see as birth and death on the earth, over time is called the seasonal transformation of life—SEASONS.

From where we stand and how we gather information, we name and order everything around us. We sometimes forget that our perspective is simply not all there is. Without stepping back and seeing the wonder of mystery, we are left categorizing all we see—thinking that what we have done has somehow helped life on earth. When we acknowledge a surrender and death into ONENESS or UNION beyond who we are, we are allowing for there to be no real answer and no real question—just simply Presence.

In a linear and organized world our faith falls down into the individual pieces of cause and effect. We trade expansion for contraction. We trade non-local for local. We trade the transcendent for the imminent. We trade a piece for the whole. Union, death, passion, grief, consumption, and surrender seek to bring it all together. The many and the ONE.

What follows are poems that were written with an eye to the experience of falling into consummation. Many of the poems were written while on retreat or vacation. They were written with enough space around my heart and mind for me to be able to perceive the Other in the now.

You have to be able to put some space between yourself and the present if you want to smash your left and right hemispheres together enough to become one with the One. You have to retreat into the immediate to find the beyond. You have to jump into the immanent to fall out into the transcendent.

+   +   +

There is often no real sense that merger or union is taking place. You are hopping from rock to rock (interacting with the descriptive layers of interpreting life) and the next thing you know, you are in the stream. Somewhere you entered the stream. You fell into the stream. You look at Orion in the morning sky of autumn, and your heart bursts into the fullness of the Milky Way. You are sitting by a deafening brook, noticing the hazy curl of white water movement around and under the rock and your soul falls in.

It happens like that. It is an instantaneous thing. And, all of the moments of tiny abandon we face in life are shards and pieces of our ultimate abandon in God.

There are times—if you are lucky, and have paid attention all along the journey—that you may feel it coming on like drifting into sleep. You enter it without a startling spasm. Most times; however this is NOT the case.

Robert Bly has spent a lot of time charting out the territory of "leaping poetry" in what became known as "deep image" poetry. He talks about a "psychic energy" that exists within the body. This energy moves about when it connects with "deep images" in poetry. Hopping from rock to rock across the stream, this psychic energy of Bly feels like it is the self/Self axis of the mystics. It is the aggregate of the person that has an "isness". In simple terms it is the "I" or the "me". When we surrender the "I" or "me" to the One, then the "psychic energy" has fallen into the stream itself and merged with the larger "I"—God.

This psychic energy is the illusory image of identity that Rumi calls us to annihilate in "fana". We tend to think that surrender or abandonment is a way that we can choose to go. According to Rumi, it is not.

Surrender is really all there is. Union is the backdrop of the ALL. Eventually, we will all come up against surrendering. It is best we learn to surrender now. Some wisdom-teachers have expressed this need to rehearse our merger and union by telling us to "die before we Die". Perform little acts of death so the big act of Death is not so foreign to us.

Poems are wormholes. They are black-holes. As we were warned by Dante in the Divine Comedy, "Abandon hope all ye who enter." We should no less recognize the death/surrender we espouse when we enter the Stream on the backs of the rocks of poetry; when we enter into union with the LORD. Our ego must writhe and scream; for, to enter the Stream is to lose the self into the Self. Give yourself away—with caution and abandon. Resurrection is sure to follow.

"What have I ever lost by dying". —Rumi

The Poems

BOAT 3.0

When I am old
I shall have a boat that
I put-out in every day.

I will bounce on waves
with little care of where
I go, but only why.

The where will not interest
me, but THAT shall.

That I should stare deep
into her depths and weep. That
I should find in her the tears
of my thousands of lives,
mingled softly and hardly
against the other cries of
anguish made from the bottom
of my lives.

That a fish would be taken
I would find ok. I would
eat her nourishment as salt
and ashes and tears as bread.

What else do you eat, when you
have arrived at the place of
looking,

the place of deeply
knowing that your pain is not
just one visit to the barber,
but it is a weeping at being
tired of being a man. Until
you can no longer be satisfied
with knowing
and must instead
stare into the blue, drag out her
morsel,
enter the ocean
and get lost in the cycle
of the boatman.

The paint that I have scraped off,
and the edges I have sanded smooth
are ready now for paint. And, when she dries,
I will push this boat back out—away from
shore, and seal the coldness of life
against the salty ocean blue.
I shall stare down
into her and
get lost.

BOAT 2.0

When I am old
I should like to sit
on the top of the water
in a boat I sand and paint
each year—
myself.

I can hear the Sea
call to me, "Come.
Sit. Stare. Come into me."

A fleck, a crumb
can only fall to the
surface for a second.
It is taken down on
the curl of a wave.

She is hungry—the Sea.
She is hungry for me.
She consumes me.

BOAT 1.0

When I am old
I should like a boat
to sand and paint
and pull through
the waves.
I will put out on the
Sea each day and
take from her the fish
she holds about my
island home.

From her place
I will do nothing.
I will not call to land
or signal to the
other boats. I will
fish and stare into
her depths and get
lost in her forever.

HIDDEN BASIN

The river sits there,
dragging itself slowly
across its rocky basin.

A branch bends back
and forth in the heavy
flow. Why has my father
folded up his courage
and put it in a drawer?
Why has he hidden his
strength in someone else's
pocket?

I cannot be
sure.

I thought at his age
he would be sitting here
solid and strong, steady
and stayed; and, in a deep
silence, reaching in to
touch the earth under
the river. Touching her
stillness with the courage
of one. Entering into
the stream and
losing himself in her.

I have felt the bottom
of the river. Will I ever
be able to share it with
him? Or, will he fade
from view and greatness
with prostatitis and
blood thinners?
Never having tasted
The ONENESS of the ONE.
The ONENESS that comes from
going deeply
into the bottom
of the river
at which he stares.

MOKSHA

I know the way the waves
come in and pound the
sand and bring her
gifts from the deep.

I have seen the way
the shells stop themselves
and lay there
belly-up and
belly-down and paint
the morning sand with love.

I have tasted the
way the brine sprays
itself across the
beach, toward
the grasses bunched
together in a dune

where everything from her
bottomless depths comes
to find itself exposed
on the surface.

Where the whole
world is washed up
on the shores of union.

NODDING

On the underside
of a gull's wing -
just below the
shoulder—an old
man sleeps; nodding
back and forth.

He sleeps,
not only on his face,
but deep in his chest.
Down in the center. He
sleeps there, too.

It is the way the
neck bends, to the
chest, to the ground,
that makes him sleep
so sleepfully sleepy -
drool running down his
mind and into the dreams
he does not know he
holds onto for every
waking breath,
dancing himself into the
mystic oneness of all
on the silver pathway
of his dreaming
dream.

SPRAY

From the table
I can sit and
feel the spray of
the Sea on my
unshaven face.

The ocean eats a
man. She eats out
his brain and leaves
only a mist—a fog.
She eats out his heart
and leaves only her
depths.

Her feeling is fuller
than mine. It is more
fluid. It crashes
and laps at me like
a billowing darkness.
It takes me away -
piece by piece—until
I am no longer. Until
I am refuse on her
swollen shores.

And I have not
left my chair.

WORDS

Sometimes, when the words
dance all around
my head
and pull the strings
attached to my feeling,
I am opened to being
at Rest.

They are there to take
me in—these words.
The geese flying
over the frozen lake
echo their cries
into my chest and
bring me joy. They
pull me in—in to my Self.

Sometimes I realize
I am not just this
body, this place of feeling.
I am not just words
nor just geese. But,
I am and am not. I am
the joy and the absence of joy.

It was then,
while watching the words
and the geese,
I realized awareness
is often confusing.

Just listen to
the echo over the lake
it will eat you alive.

A FEATHERED WING

The dipping of
a feathered wing
into the snow
into the hill
has caused a stirring
in my heart.
I did not see
exactly how it happened

but we never do.

The moon charts her course
on tracks I cannot see.

The trout circles the frog on her
plotted course—a course
I know nothing of. And in an
instant the frog is gone; the
moon has fallen; and my heart
is afire with the motion of a
feather I did not see and
did not feel.
The entrance
Into One
Is often
Missed

We simply show up
And have no notice
Of our arriving.

SWEET-KISSING

Tenderness begins in the place
where two faces meet;
In the space where two
lives come together.

There is a silence, a
thundering silence bedecked
with silvery trim. That is
how it is marked as sacred.

A mother holds her child
to her face. A doe licks the
muzzle of her fawn. The
eagle brings torn and bloodied
muscle to her eaglet.

One consumes the other
And other consumes the One.

It turns like this,
the world does.
Moving closer in
on itself. It is we
who sometimes miss
the merger. The sun
is always rising, and
setting. It is we who
sometimes obscure it
from our view with a
hand.

And when the child
tilts his head, and
when the mother cranes
her neck this
consuming-kissing
is great sweetness;
this kissing is
tenderness unveiled.

A SPIRITUAL FATHER'S FATHER

This praying,
it turns on a papa's knees.

Veiling my life in
its warmth.

His fingers
entwined with mine -
wrapped over and under -
gnarling wisteria gathered
together and becoming one.

This man,
he taught me the words
to God, to His Mother.
He has taught me to bloom
from the belly—loudly -
and to be heard
from here—this monastic hall -
in my prayers.

This blooming,
it has worked its way
into me and has opened
my heart to all of this:
to this place men's prayers,
to this place of angel's words,
to this place of candle lit silence
and Oneness with the unspeakable.

All that this heart has become
is entwined in the wisteria
of his strong hands and heart
of stillness.

STARKNESS

There is a certain
quality to starkness -
to the crying of
the winter wind.

I suppose
it is the grayness
of standing on a cliff,
overlooking a
purple river
surrounded
by leafless trees.

The bareness
betrays a unity
sown
together by the howling
and ripping of
the cold air through
the river valley.

Two feathers
blow helplessly
on the end of my staff.
And, the cold, cold
wind numbs my ears -
from the top all the way
around to the lobe.

MOTHS AND ANGELS

When the lash of an angel
brushed my cheek
I saw the world through
new eyes.

It was a reflection
riding
on the water's surface;
the place
where two pieces
of wood come together—joining.

That is how it comes to you.

There may be no words
to herald the opening.
One minute the tomb is sealed
and the next,
the stone
is rolled away.

When it stops,
hitting the far wall,
it disturbs a moth—so tiny,
so weak—
flitting about.

A delicate feather
from the small moths wing,

floats to the ground,
to the moss,
and settles within.

I have seen that. My life has had
its meaning there.

There.
And I have lived in that.
Mottled oneness.

But, for an instant.

CHAPEL CHILL

The wind howls
a chill,

hugging the
walls as she dances.

The pipes hiss and
rattle,
bringing their heat to
this chapel chill.

Poem and petition
race back and forth
on the beat of
the heart
and the trail of the
senses . . . and I sit,

enshrouded by the arms
of this place of men,
and of angels,
and of silence.

Called inside
I am nothing.
the space between us
melts into mystic
union of all

and there is nothing
left behind in
our prayers.

The floor is so clean here.

COLD BRICKS OF WISDOM

The wind howls,

whipping over
the surface of the
stone,

wrapping her limbs
coldly around
the building's bricks.

I feel her all
over the walls like
tongues of ice
retreating in long
slow licks.

My neck chills
and shivers when
she chants
her wail.
I know
She is here.
I cannot see Her,
but O how I
know She is here,
slowing me down
to a frozen stillness
just before the "one-ing"
of me
with her.

FLOWER HEART

Does the daffodil
hear
the buzzing
of the bee?

He comes to her
and
makes love to her.

Their sweetness
on our tongue,
a honeyed-union
of quiet relish
and closed eyes.

Our eyes tell our
hearts to be still.
He is gone.
She has faded.
But, I.

LAKE AMBLESIDE

I could stand
and stare at the lake -
this lake -
and get lost in her.

Paddled under
On the broken leg
of a swan
to become the horn -
that fallen to the bottom
as dirt—
becomes a mountain,
rising upward,
a trumpeting presence
to surround and
to protect her.
I bring the water in -
fresh and cool -
on the rivers.

Refreshing her and
feeding her every
second of her
beauty and depth.
She has merged
with my core.

I could stand
and stare at her

all my life—
and get lost forever
right now.

FLECKS AND SCALES

I have put myself
on that wave
over there
on the other side.

The wave with the small amber
flecks and faded scales
of the great cold salmon.

I have put myself there
to feel
a different feeling
from the scratch and burn
of woolen chairs and forced heat
all around me in my comfortable
home of apathy.

To take myself closer to
things we have not made ourselves.
To the other in the other over there.

I pull close to me the
flecks and scales. Push
into me these bitty treasures
of the deep and the shallow;
the shallow and the deep. Plant
them in me to grow.

Suspended and released,
the water holds them
and moves them with an
orchestrated randomness
that mocks our best
attempts to measure
and hold and shape.

Dance and stillness meld
into a display of
inexpressible rhythm.
I am whirled into oneness
With that fish.

Fallen apart
One scale
At a time.

I've put that in me
and it cannot be taken
away. It has been growing
there, out of control, for
years;

even before
I planted it. It is
a gathering together
of the pieces –
a "ONE-ING" of my
own self.

ALL ALONG

I must put my foot down
on the heather by the brook.
I must stand on the hill
where the castle is falling down.
I must stare into the sea from
a place on the sanded shore.
I must keep my feet on Scottish
greening soil.

You cannot know
the power that comes
up out of the earth -
wrapping itself
around your foot
and leg, dragging you
into its belly -
unless you change places.
You must leave your land,
depart from your home,
and go across the waters
of time and space
and feel the dirt
of another's place.

It is then,
in this new connection,

you will know you have
been there a thousand,
thousand times before.

Without moving
you will never know
you have been there—
consuming and consumed -

all along.

LIKE THAT

If I could just lay down
on that rock—

right on that shag moss -
the moss right where the
dew is—

if I could just lay
down there, I could sleep
like a badger in a hawk-less
land. All stretched out and
melted in the careless sun.

If I could just tuck my head
under my arm—

behind my
back like a duck cranes its
neck around, to hide its beak -

if I could just tuck my head
like that, I could float forever
on the listless waters.

This body does this.

It sees those things
outside itself—those
things that are other -

over there, and it sends
itself out,
out there

to mingle.

Mingled with the grasses,
twigs, rocks, hares, and
hawks I am a rose and
then the peat. I am a trout
and then the river.

Ah, and
once I thought I was only
these limbs—these limbs
that carry my changing form.
But now, I have become
all things.

I consume and am consumed.

I know what
Taliesin sang for.
He sang for union.

PULLING DOWN LIGHT

It is the way the autumn
leaves
pull the light down
  to the ground
that I have been noticing lately.

It comes to be the same with
  all dyings,
with all deaths. Just before
we merge into the ONE
we burst into flame.

It is the way they reflect their brightness
  to the corners of my eyes -
    These golden maples and red –

their dappled colors to my heart.

That is the way their dying goes.

Pulling down
  great bunches of the light
  right before
  they fall
to the ground
and die and become the earth
upon which we all stand.

OPENING IN THE HEART

There is an opening
in the heart
for tears.

It is on
the top, left side.

There is
an opening in the heart
for sweat, too.

It is along
the back.

There is a place
where it all
comes together
into oneness.

And all the
blood that flows through
us is added to by
this sadness and
this work.

Love is watered down
with sorrow and effort;
watered down

into an aching hollow
openness for holding
and being held.

Our days pour down into the
heart
where we eat
and are eaten by
all that is and Him.

Toil and travail work
their way into
our every heartbeat –
union come by
grace and striving.

It has taken me
a lifetime to know
how to say this.

SLIPPING AWAY AGAIN: GOD AND YET ANOTHER HOSPICE PATIENT

You are slipping away
again. You are dying in yet another
body. You lay here for
me to visit with.

You, the countless shifter
of faces and lives.

You are ebbing out of
consciousness again.

Going to that place
inside your form,
that place of quiet rest
and stillness where
you consume and
are consumed.

Your face is becoming
the same again.

On yet another body,
it looks remarkably the same.

Your eyes roll up inside
their sockets.
Your mouth hangs open,
breathing from the chest -
almost gasping.

Your skin gets cold
and then hot
again and again and again.
And, it looks and feels
like tallow again.

And them, all of them
that have come to hold
your hand and
tell you that they love you,
they are all in pain
and so unsure, again.

You have pulled so inside
yourself
that you are unfamiliar
to them
and they are scared.

I have seen you pull
inside and leave
a thousand, thousand
times and it is always
the same.

Again, and again, and
again.

And yet,
you will appear anew

again and again and again

in the unfolding of yellow
daffodil flesh
in the spring

and in the
rattling cry of the
newborn child.

STILLNESS IN THE WOOD

Echoing
Off the heavy air

a wing flaps
behind my ear.

I am amazed
at the blanketed
sound that muffles
motion and movement
across the snow
in the grayness
of the winter's day.

A hollow echo
consumes me
in its surrounding.

An owl
in a tree -
at a distance -
sits still
wrapped
in soundlessness
and wonder

somehow one with all
with me.

That silent distance
in the snow and
air
bring together
the whole terrain

one family
in the chest -
in the heart.

The silence
and the echoed
stillness in
the snowy woods
gives us a chance
for me to feel at one
with all I see
in the muffled
me-ness
of the horizon of God
jutting out of my heart
onto the landscape of
snow,
and owl,
and white draped trees.

FROZEN FALLINGS

Ice falls from the trees,
crashing to the ground,
breaking into pieces
of forgotten fullness.

As it melts
into the frozen surface
of the earth,
it is lost
to something much
much larger.

How can we expect anything less.

MOON RAYS

I looked for the strong
rays of the moon
the night we anointed
you with myrrh.

Even a soft glow would
have given me strength.
There was no moon -
there was no strength.

I wanted to tell you how
beautiful the moon is:
how she is full of energy
for the dark side
for the soft side.

I remember first seeing
your arms—fresh dandelion
stems moving—moving
about your sides.
You brought us such joy.

I wanted to walk with
you in the daffodil
fields by our first home,
teach you how to hold
a butterfly on your
finger, and let
you eat clover with
the rabbits.

The tea we would have had,
made with peppermint leaves
from our garden,
would have made you smile -
feeling its tingle and honeyed
sweetness in your mouth.

Hand in hand we would
have walked the sands
while the mother-waters
crashed on the beach and
the sun put itself to bed -
glowing ourselves
with a powerful peace
and cheer.

I want you to stay with us,
Zoe Alexandra,
and join our circle
of love
as we taste the earth,
touch beauty, and dance through
separating pains.

But you cannot.

And now,
I feel my life being
eaten by a grief

whose edges I cannot
see—I have
no map of where
I am going. I
am set aside to
be consumed.

THE EYE OF THE NEEDLE

The conditions
of our heart
arise and fall,
arise and fall.

One moment at play with
the subtleties of gentleness
another with the
"harshnesses" of anger.

It takes
just the right
moment—

an opening -

for us to be hungry
for grace,

to be hungry
for repentance,

and for us to
receive the mercies
of God

that are ever-pouring
through the needle's
eye

into our lives.

Eternity is
there,
streaming through the
needle's eye

will we enter in,
will we bask in its rays?

Open to consuming
power of union.
It can annihilate
you.

A WAVE—HALF CAPTURED BY THE OCEAN

How can
the I
remove my
obsession with
the my and
release the
grasp of its
own
little
ego-self.

A wave
half captured
by the ocean
cannot return
to the lonely
smallness of
its single self.

A ray
shining forth
from the
light-heat-burning
mass of
the sun
cannot
be itself
without the
star.

Back
and forth,

between the little
and the big,
between the one
and the many

the heart
beats on

grasping
and releasing
and getting lost.

THE TEARS THE DARK SKY CRIED

The rain falls heavy
on the ground
around our home,

carving rivulets
down to the lake,
down to the stream
just below.

I have heard
the tears
the dark sky cried

all night

breaking into the snow,
taking ice
from the roofs
and landing in
puddle after puddle
a colding mud.

The wind has now come
to set the tears
on edge,

and I am left
warm inside
carving words
from the air

and sipping coffee
as the day
and my rest
grow old –
Hoping for a chance to
get lost in the mud
of God.

HARDENING

The heart has wounds all around it.

Places where arrows once
tore and bloodied muscle.

They have healed since then,
turning gray-brown, flat
not giving or returning
when poked with a finger.

Some trees turn to stone.
A curious thing. They
just up and become some
other thing. They become
some thing else.

Pieces
of me have turned to stone.
The dead pieces.
Mostly the wounds
around the heart.

There are other place too,
just below my ass, where
I used to welt up after
a belting. That turned to
pine and then
to stone. My little toe
is still turning from wood

to stone. I don't know why,
but it is all twisted—all
humped up. It is becoming
a statue.

At times
I feel the top of my
back—the field between
my shoulders—hunching up.
A swelling mountain
pushing through the skin.
That one I think I'll stop.
But who knows.

Trees that turn to stone
are a curious thing.
The body has dead men
all around it. People who
have once lived,
or maybe not.

They walked with me
and I have spoken
with them, but the hollow
behind their eyes would
not let them raise a fist
and yell with me. They
softened. They became
jelly.

At some point,
when I was not looking -
or maybe I was -
the hand and the fist
crumbled, the jelly glued
shut the lid. No more air
could enter; and they
too were stone.

Can anything stop this
constant turning of things
into stone?

This turning to stone
is a curious thing.
It works against
the hunger my heart
has to swallow God
and be eaten alive
by Him.

It works against
the tender softening
that opens my edges
to assume the Presence
of the ALL.

The expansion
of the heart that knows

no hardening is
the entrance into the
a union with the
holy fleck of all
that is—a universe
in a mote
of dust.

MORNING PRAYER

The cool stillness
of the morning abbey
soaks the prayers into
me as warmth and heat.

There is a pause, here;
there is a pause
between the words,
between the lines
of mourning;

the lines of prayer;
the lines of beseeching.

I used to think the words were the
prayer; today,
and perhaps

through all time,
it is the pause.
The pause
takes me in
to the ever-expanding
encroachment of the
Holy and Divine One
lurking on the edges
of my life –

waiting to snatch me up.

THE TREES CHANT

The wind
blows steady
over the surface of
the frozen lake.

From the hills
it carries the sound
of trees chanting
the chants
of the monks
of old.

Gregorian tunes
mingle with the
rattle of leaf on
leaf.

If you hold your
heart still
in the gray morning
hours, even the
cry of the hawk
rises as a prayer

like incense
to the nose of
the ALL-WISE.

An aroma of
piety
and song—of
salvation and bliss
blows in across
the stillness
of the frozen lake.

Blows in and sets
us free to know
that all of this
is also a part
of WE, a part
of ME.

ONE YEAR

Last year
at this same time
we were packing
to go to Greece.

The islands of
honey and stone

left the ocean, and basil, and
olives in our soul.

Tinos held the smell
of warm sun -
baked chamomile, growing
between the earth and
veins of green marble.

Aegina left
 the shaded home
of olive orchards
and Cyprus trees.
And now,
now I am cut in
half with pain.

O Virgin,
O Nectarios,
what has happened?

Who chose to blow our
world apart and steal
our little girl-gift
from Glinda's womb.

Who did not choose -
did not choose to help.

All I see
passing before the eyes of
my heart are
the churches,
the seaside,
the taverns,
and the tired
worn people of the
earth; of the faith.
How happy we were;
how full of joy, and
oil and wine and mirth.

How dry our hearts were;
dry of tears and filled with
laughter and sex.

That joy,
that joy now
lets me weep;
cuts me in half to weep.

Grieving,
grieving,
grief.

The harrowing beauty of
the small hearty flowers and
strong gnarly herbs of that
place, and our joy
lets me,
no,
makes me weep.

NO MORE MYTH

What happens when
myths stop coming up
out of the ground?

A great fire-bird does not
come out of the traveling sun.

A crane no longer hangs
above the lake.

A clump of growth that
hangs over a crack in the
cement is a weed.

Extracted from the earth
is a story, the heart
has no place.

Wandering,
the spirits are wandering.

The microscope gives us
our answer and the camera
removes all doubt.

There is nothing to tell
around the fire, but
random tragedies,
rampant destructions,
fascinating facts.

No hungry God
waits to eat His progeny.
No man stalks the Divine beast.

Dissolve imagination,
shut out dreams,
stop making tales.

There is no need for poems,
or for stories, or for the making
of myths.

Community is gone
and woven tales are no longer
permitted to come out
of the earth.

No one ever says
they were
eaten by God. No
one ever boasts
that they ground
the God-meat with
their teeth.

We have lost
our tales
of "one-ing".

MINGLED

It is coming up through me
from the ground.
My feet are pulling it
out of the earth -
tearing it
from the dirt.

It is dark,
silvery,
heavy and full
of power.

My heart beats with it
these days.
It courses through
all my veins -
ivory growing from bone
and iron deposits in the
hot and cooling core.
It bubbles.

There is no joy
in this grief
that comes from
the dirt,
that comes from
the ground
and from death.

There is rest
sometimes,
but there is no joy.

It mingles with me
and falls down again.
Trying to pull me
back in to its depths.
I pull to keep myself
from going in,
from going under.

My pulling
and its
pulling get
lost and mixed
together and
unclear. Who is
pulling which and
which whom?

Traces of silvery pools
mix with blood and seep
into the crevices of
the cracked dirt.
No tree will grow here,
no blade of grass.

Only the buzzards
and the ravens
will come here
and peck at the soil;
tasting for death
between the broken
earth and the pieces
of bloodied gravel.

A THOUSAND YEARS OF STARING

The smell of wood
burning in the fireplace
dances in the air
mixing with the
sound of the river.

Today, I am sure
we learned about motion
by watching the water.

Thousands of years of staring,
daily staring,
heavy staring,
into the flowing
wetness –

driven moisture –

made them sure they
could float a log
or turn a wheel.

I have come here for
the sound of her movement,
for the peace of
her traveling—to hide from
Zoe's death.

The geese come here.
They move at sunset,

as the glow disappears,
a chorus swells.

One goose
carries the point of
the song;
pounding home the call
to make music.
"Sing. Sing," she calls.
And, they do.

A lovely song.
It grows and deepens
as they approach.
And, as they are overhead,
I close my eyes, and
with Rumi, I raise my
hand and drink in
the secret nectar.

I dance.
Twirl,
pause,
slide, whirl.
I have come here
for the geese.

I have come here
for them to sing
the song for me.

This past week
our little girl died.

Zoe Alexander,
laden with cysts on
her head and spine,
died inside her mother.

We saw her on the
screen. Little hands and feet.
A chord, and cysts. Before
they could take her from us,
she died.

I came to the river to
stare. My numbness screams
out to listen. I came here to
hear the geese. Here
there are no words of consolation,
no words of hope; but,
the pounding of the silence
and the movement.

I came to the river
That the one goose might carry
The point of the song for me.
For now, I must stare, and feel
the pounding rhythm of darkling flow
within my arches, within my chest.
I am consumed.

TEAR CLOUDS

The clouds held rain
like our tears -

heavy beyond holding.
For days they spilled
out of our eyes,
over our lids,
down our cheeks
in unending streams of warmth.

O God,
how,
even when we had stopped
crying, how they did run
out, slopping over the sides
of our bucketed hearts.
Never-ending.

I cannot
form the questions.

The mind has ceased
and the heart has
joined forces with
the body.

The mind's grief is confusion.

Its grief is not the grief of
the rest of the body -

those wrenching, twisted
knotted aches.

It is more
a still grief.

Unsure and childish.

The body mourns and mourns
and mourns, becoming empty
and endlessly full,
changing the course
of life -

Never to be the same again.
The mind grieves confusion.

The heart holds hands with the
body and pours out its grief
onto the rutted
earth that is grooved
by the soul of time forever.

Weather changing deeply,
clouds moving endlessly to the
rhythm of drenching and drying;
digging trenches in soft feeling
that screams in pain.

THE OTHER SIDE

There is another side
to every snow-bank.
The place the wind
could not touch,
did not reach and
pile snow in
random patterns of cold.

It is quiet there.
There is little noise
and the muffled
stillness sings warmly
to the heart.

There is an underside
to the surface of the lake -
to the surface of the pond.
The duck and goose
paddle under all that come
from above

paddle it down to
that place on the
water's bottom where

there is little noise
and the muffled
stillness sing darkly
to the heart.

This inward thing -
this other side to
the snow-bank,
this underside of
the surface of
things

this is a place
so close that it
is far, far away.

Our heart is
just below the
skin,
just below the
bone,
but it takes
a journey to
Byzantium to unlock
the final membrane
of remembrance.

It is that other side,
it is that under side
where all the empty
fullness dances and swirls
like a flake in a
whirlwind
and a speck on the
current.

A sparrow flits
and breaks the concentration,
an acorn falls
and the attention
is brought back
to now. And the stillness
awaits a traveler from
another day.

It is all One
in the thousand
faces of the many.

EMPTINESS

There is an emptiness in me
that cannot form words

or even hear them.

A crack in the macadam
with not even a weed -
unwanted thing -
poking through to the sun.

It may be because our
child is now dead;

or because this is the
time in the mottled and damp
green-brown world
for no stirrings.

Nothing moves but birds
on the top, scouring
the moist earth for worms
to pull up from the dirt.
Scabs from the skin.

Pre-spring death just hangs
dank,

blends with silhouettes
and with the ground
and just stays there.

Slowly. Slowly the birds
will bring back the daffodil's
yellow, the tulip's red, and
the skies lion blue.

Slowly
the crocus will push up,
burst and fade to milky
white. When this has come,
perhaps by then, words
will return. Words that feel
as if they have meaning.

ELIXIR

I know what the silver
elixir was.

The drink I stole and
consumed to slake
my thirst.

It was grief;
and O how it
burned out my soul
and ran through my body,
out of my toes,
onto my sandals.

It came to me
A week ago in a dream -
posing as a drink
I was told I should not
drink.

O mercurial elixir,
O burning change.
I know what the silver elixir was.
It was Zoe and the alchemy of
hellish change that has begun.
I am lost
in a delirium
to something so much
larger than I.

I am swallowed
by grief –

in God.

ONE SECOND

It only takes one second
for the soul to leave the body.

A flicker on the screen,
a tightening of the face
and it drains right out.

From the head-
through the heart-
out of the feet-
onto the highly polished
gray flecked white
linoleum floor.

The pathways of ecstasy
become vacant,

the heart becomes hollow,
and the mind numbed
becomes one-pointedly empty.

Gone;
hope, joy, elation.

It only takes one second
for the soul to leave the body.

This is the same
time it takes

to be overshadowed by
bliss: for the
SPIRIT to fill the body.

I have stood
on the banks of
grief, love and ecstasy

and I am
beginning to feel
that there is
not as much
of

a difference
as I had once
hoped that
there was.

In any case,
I am
lost
and
consumed
by the
ONE that
stalks me.

INTO THE EARTH

Snow melts
into the earth

and dirt swells
gladly

holding it
for the sun's passing.

Drinking from
these

fresh streams

can only come
by dying.

LIGHT FROM THE MOON

The light rays
hidden behind the clouds
come down to me in cool,
grey reflection

lighting the snow
at my feet,
making a path
for me to walk.

A call from
the woods gives
me pause to wonder

how do we survive
against all odds
and lean into the
frozen banks

of snow

the frozen banks of
places in our lives
that have become
like ice -
able to preserve
us and keep

us until a thaw
is possible,

until a thaw is
attainable.

I remember
pain that was
too great to bear

that with the safety
of days and weeks

emerged to be
felt -

when a clearing around
the swift
onset
had been made.

A family slowly
coming undone,

a doctor telling
us there was nothing
left to do,

a father lying still
and alone on a
hospital table -

waiting to be
identified.

These spaces that grow
around pain are
sometimes missed,

The light that
exposes them is subtle.

It is a great gift
to be the subtle light

illuminating the stillness
and a place to come
undone, in the
safety of friends
and love.

It is this light
that often saves us.

It is this light
That is our true selves,
The self that
illumines,
suffuses,
and merges
with all it touches –
with all it reveals.

THE PEARL OF THE HEART

Having come
to the water's
edge -

the farside
banks of the
great ocean
of days -

I have
shed all
that would
hold me back.

And climbing
down from the
heights of thought,

I have plunged into
the abyss of life
and searched

for the light
that would
rid me of
all darkness.

Hidden
deep

within the
depths of the sea

I found a shell
that was hard to
open -

my heart has
been made known -

its beauty
revealed with
the flash
of a blade.

O blessed
love,
O divine glory

the silent peace
that glows from
this jewel

has taken me across
the expanse of
days

and has enlivened
my being.

Stillness
covers me as
with a blanket.

Silence cries
out and deafens me.

O holy gem;
O priceless jewel
deliver me from
my poverty

and clothe me with
your righteousness.

Clothe me with the
blue oneness of
your pulsing
being.

PRUNING THE HEART

I am pruning
the limbs of my heart
today.

I am finding the branches
that have no life,
have no ability
to support new growth,

and taking them away.

There is a fire
in my heart that will
burn their dryness.

I take these
clippings to
that place.

Throwing them
on the embers
stokes the fire
and fans the warmth.

That which is dead
will burn and glow

turning waste into
food, turning emptiness
into fullness.

When I was younger
I could carry all
of this dead wood

around with me
and feel no pain.

Today, I have
need to lighten the
load

and fuel the desires of love
and compassion.

In their removal
I am not diminished

I am enlivened.

Burn, fire burn.
Fill me with
Light and Warmth,

Baptized anew with
the Spirit's flame.

Standing this close
I can only hope
that all will be consumed
by the radiant awe of
the wonderful One.

BECKONING

Beckoning
from the cold,
empty
place that

sometimes rises
in my soul.

I call out -
not knowing
but
trusting
I will see
a face.

Trusting
I will hear
a voice.

The heart
alights at the
hope of encounter,
the mind is
put to ease.

A stillness
blows over the
barren, snow -

only the snow,

and in that
cold, cold
wind

is the warmth of
feeling that

all shall be well,
all shall be well,
all manner of things
shall be well.

I cannot give this to
my mind,
it races a thousand
thousand directions.

But creeping,
slowly seeping
out of my heart
is a sure sense
that the ONE will
be here.

And in that epiphany,

the mind is settled
choosing not to ride
its daunting waves
and peace comes

catching me in its
sure strong hands.

It is a path
I can only enter
by beckoning,
by crying out in my despair:
"Take me I am Yours".

THE HOLY FIRE

The path unfolds
before me,
the journey lies ahead.

I cannot see the
turns and hills, but
I know the road
will not be easy.

This time,
this dark joy,
is the cassock
of my faith.

Look upon
the suffering we
imagine
and find within the
door onto paradise.

It is here,
on this lonely
road of Lent
we travel to the
inexpressible LIGHT.

We uncover the pieces
of our ash just as
the phoenix climbs
out renewed.

We step back for
a season -
to venture a gaze into
all that we feel is
human,

is heavy and
burdensome to carry,

namely our separation
and we rise up
triumphant

realizing that we
are not two

but one,

if only we would -

if we only would.

Heaven comes to earth,
earth is raised to heaven
and when they meet—then -
only then
can we see that they have
never been two.

Open our eyes to
see the marriage in
Your Kingdom;

open our hearts to
sense that
God is with us.

As we bow down
in humility and ash,

raise us up
to burn
with the HOLY FIRE -

aflame with love.

HERE NOW

I have seen the
snowfall on a thousand,
thousand nights

but none
so exquisite
as
this -
now.

My heart often
clambers for
something to hold on to -
a memory from the past,
a story from some
other traveler.

To stand here,
now

takes far more courage
than all the
rememberings of this
one life, this one man.

Standing here, now
I must lose it all.

I am at one with the ONE.

SUBTLE CHANGES IN THE HEART

The subtle changes
in each heart
are known by scent.

A leaf turns
in the wind,

on one tree it rattles -
on another it does not.

A kicked stone
tumbles along its path.

One bounces left
another right.

Sometimes I would
like to know—with my mind -
with my reasoning self

what the differences are
between each person.
If one is true,
if another is simple,
another is an enemy.

Mostly
it is something
that my inside scent
just picks up.

In my ordered world
this is a gift;

in the kingdom of grace
I must lay it aside.

The path across the lake
shifts with each gust of wind.

Sometimes it is hidden all together.
We are still expected
to travel across the ice.

I KNOW

I know what is
written on the underside
of the rocks.

The rocks that sit
on the bottom of the lakes,
that lay scattered
throughout the creek beds
on all the earth.

It is stillness.
It is love.

Quietly clinging
to the surface of
the stones
stillness and love
call out to us

asking us to
take them in,
make them a home,
shelter them.

Can I find the
space in my laden-full
heart to hold two
more things -

two things that will
set me free.

I reach into the
pool of life's
waters and I
gaze on the gifts
of the deep.

Today they are
mine.

NITRIA AND SKETIS

They wandered to the desert
seeking solitude—to be
alone with the Alone.

Even there they had
to fight to find stillness.

The world followed
them to obtain their
pearl of great price.

Deeper and deeper into
the desert they fled,

always still just a few feet
away from the hungering hordes.

The price for solitude is high -
it is your life. The cost of
stillness is everything.

And then,
when you find it,

you must give it away;
it is never yours alone.

Piercing into the Heart
of God is a culinary
delight that is to be
shared around the
Table of Life.

There is no
secret eating.

The manna cannot
be stored in
earthen vessels for

more than just
that day's meals -
that day's feasts.

WAITING FOR LENT

The stillness in the
morning pink is grey
with waiting -

waiting for the snow,
waiting for the winds,
waiting for Lent.

The days are
numbered with
a hazy abstinence

some will turn
away foods, others
will turn away drinks,
can we turn away
the ego.

Fighting for its
position in our
lives,
in our hearts,
this tool
of survival is
to be laid down
so we may receive the
greatest tool of all -
the SPIRIT.

The morning is
waiting for that.

Lent is waiting for that.

In the quiet
dawning of the
sun,

a tiny bird
lands on a
branch,

hungry for a seed.

I want to be
that hungry.

WE DO NOT

There is a waiting
in the heart -

a waiting for
that next big thing

the next big opening
into growth and
expansion.

There is a waiting
in the heart -

a desire to join
our smallness
with all that is.

Sometimes we
imagine this when
we buy that next thing -

it will remove from
us all of our smallness

all of our broken
pettiness and darkness.

If we could just get that
one thing, we would
be whole at last -

we would be whole
again.

We all ready
have that wholeness

it is in the small
quiet recesses of
the heart itself.

The desire is to
be used to go there -

go to the place
we already own.

And, we do not.

IN THE WIND

I hear more in the
trees tonight

than the wind.

I hear freedom
a cleansing
cold wave that

takes from us
the burden

of our much-toiling
flesh.

I hear the silence
behind the ocean

of pine whipping
sound,

bough whistling
peace -

a peace
that knows it is
all.

It passes
more than just
all understanding.

It passes
all beauty,
all joy,

even all hope.

Because it is
all of these things.

And how is it
that the wind

in a simple turning
of Oneness

can be all of these things -
freedom, peace, understanding,
beauty, joy and even hope.

That
I may never know.

But, I hear it.

I OWN THE STARS TONIGHT

I own the stars
tonight

I reach out and
they are mine

I can pull them
into my eyes,

into my heart for
as long as
I would like them to stay

and be the me that is
here and there,

ALL at once.

DANCE OF THE ONE

One sound
simple
soft and subtle

can take our heart
into unknown lands.

A bird

calling from its
perch in the
tree

over head
can cause a
turn in

the glance

and seeing
the eyes
of the
tufted
feathered
fowl

drops the
feeling

into the heart
and
you are gone

wrapped in awe,
in wonder,

in radical
amazement.

The fear
that is in
a grain of sand

and a handful
of dust
tips the world
into a rhythmic
dance

the dance
of oneness.

You may
never know
when it will
happen next –
Stay lost now—
forever.

FEEDING THE DIVINE

Everyday
the church cries
out the same
simple notes

the same
cry of
the heart

oh God,
come to my assistance

oh LORD,
make haste to help me.

Centuries turn
on centuries
and words and hearts clamber
to be seen,
clamber to be heard.

Can I make my
words climb
to heaven.

Can I strain
my song
enough to
be heard.

It is in the
quietude and
simplicity
of the chant

that its sound
echoes
throughout the
ages -

through all eternity.

It is in the
beating of the heart
and its feeling
that these words,
this hymn,
this chant

are carried
aloft
to the ONE

that MYSTERIUM
TREMENDUM.

They
are the words
that feed our GOD;

the words
that nourish
our LORD,
just before He
eats us WHOLE.

ACROSS THE SURFACE

Across the surface
of the frozen waters
comes the groaning
of the ice.

At first
I never
know what it is -

that sound
that is a walrus
grunt or seals'
groan or
whales' moan

takes

just a second
or two
to make sense.

The moaning
and the echoes
in the night

are ghostly
calls

specter calls

one voice
unto another.

Deep calls
unto deep at
the noise of
Your waterfalls;

All Your waves
and billows have

gone over me.

Washed in the
awe-rich
caverns of sound

a minor key
sings in
my heart,

a note of wonder
as all creation
groans –
a groan in a minor
key that weaves my heart into
the solemn echo
of a mourning mass
of matter.

DREAM SLEEP

I have heard them talk
about the haze between
the states of sleep,
the veil between
the worlds.

This fog is my
unknowing of the
world, my
unknowing of the
Divine.

Seeking,
always turning
over leaves, and stones,
and rocks;

ever looking
for the one word that will
give meaning

to the phrase of life
I cannot interpret.

I try to train
my mind

to learn the language
of the dream,

but it alludes me
and is left

as a simple,
warm feeling
in my heart and
mind.

My unknowing—by
feeling—becomes
my knowing.

Sense it,
its presence
will tell you all.

SOPHIA

She has been here
with us,
haven't you noticed.

She was speaking
from the rattle and
the hiss inside the
belly of the chapel.
She said,
"Go inside".

She was dancing for us
in the silent turning,
the whispered curving,
of the grains in the wood of the
refectory tables. She danced,
"Turn within".

She was assailing our noses with
the sweet then pungent curling wafts
of smoke, billowing up from the
warming ceramic bowl. In the clouds
she beckoned, "Go within".

She screamed
from the glaze on the
chalice, she croaked
from the glare
on the paten, "This is my Son.

He is going there,
follow Him.
It is this One
I wanted you to find,
all along".

She was in the eyes,
and in the smiles,
and the early morning
hair of everyone
who came here looking.
And all the while,
she teased us all,
"Go within.
He is there. Go within".

WATER RUNS DOWN

Water runs down.

Everywhere
down

lower,
to the lakes,
to the creeks,
to the swamps and marshes.

From one
gathering place to
another,

the water runs down.

The dirt in the
ground is heavy with
the sound of rushing
waters.

The dirt sings
"water-songs"
this time of
the year.
Cold songs.
Clean songs.
Fresh songs.

Water songs.

Listen,
ever
so gently and hear
it

It is flowing
under your feet,

under your lives.

The water that
will crack open
the daffodils,

force out the snowdrops
and trout lilies,
and awaken
the skunk cabbage

that water
has come.

Listen
to its song and
be filled with joy.

The flowers of spring
have again
begun their
returning.

We are refreshed
once more,
bathed
in the chilling cold
of the running water
and in the ocean of
buds and blossoms that
will flow
across our paths,

into our eyes,

and straight
into our hearts.

THE HEART LONGS

How the heart longs
for a peace unending,
for joy in a friendship
with God.
For a Oneness with
The ONE.

It longs for an end
to strife and divided lives.

A bird lands
in the nest
and feeds the young
with all that it has gathered.

The heart sinks into saying,
YES. This is as it should be.

A bear takes its young
with it for a season
maybe two. Turning over
logs and digging through
the ants, licking them up.

It shares its berries and
its grub. The heart feels
YES again.

But we
cannot
sit around a table
of faith without
finding diversions that
should not be. Paying the
mortgage for the too large
building,

collecting more from the
burdened souls that come
to pray
to eat God
to care for the poor.

There can be no teaching
the young to hunger
and thirst for righteousness
when our faith has become
a project, managed to avoid

waste and undue
expense. We have turned
our Father's House into
a den of thieves and robbers.

How the heart longs
for a peace unending.

It longs for an end
to strife and divided lives.

The heart longs
to be opened by
God, to make
a place for the
King to dwell.

Listen then to the
needs of the heart.
Do not allow
anything else to rule.

Where there are leaders
who call for fiscal reform,
ignore them.

Where there are practical
men who want to build
larger buildings, assail them
with these words:

"I long for YOU."
"Don't bring ME any more
worthless grain offerings.
Your incense is disgusting to me,
so are your New Moon Festivals,
your days of worship,

and the assemblies you call.
I can't stand your evil assemblies."

It is time
for the harvest
there can be
no more dawdling.

The heart knows what
it wants, it longs
for and hopes for
things we have forgotten
to mention.

Find those things.
Seek those things.
Ask for those things.

Be filled with
what can satisfy.

Consume nothing less
than the Consumer of souls.

IT SEEMS THE SNOW IS GOING

It seems the snow is going.
It is not.
It is changing.

The flakes are no longer
alone

by themselves

but melded into one.

They have
become water
that seeps into

the earth

falling
one drop
at a time
from the ice
hanging
on the corners of my home.

They have not left.
They are here

only different,
only new,
waiting to be
birthed again
from the clouds that
call them home.

Today.
Tomorrow.

Again.

RAIN

The rain is
giving nurse to hundreds
of small lives
that lie just
below the surface
of the decomposing leaves
and loam of last
year's birth and death.

You can almost
hear them pushing their
way through the dirt -

toward the air that will
give them a second
breath, a gasp
of air and sunlight.

Washed clean
and fresh by
the ample bath
of moisture from
the skies
the earth children
raise their heads in
praise of the
Silent One who
commands their coming -

this year and again.

Thousands of manifest
forms
emerge from the Oneness
of the All –

this year and again.

ALL DISAPPEARING

The houses
along the hillside
are all disappearing
behind
a slow
emergence of
leaves on the
budding trees.

The haze of purpling-pink
is veiling everything
one bloom at a time.

Soon, the greening
leaves will hide even
the dirt of the hills
on which the trees stand -
holding them in place.

In two weeks the
mountains will appear
as lumbering isolates
with no dwellers,
no life other
than the trees.

Behind this
illusion, live the
people of the hills.

Seemingly invisible
soldiers of the woods.

The universe's cycle
ebbs and flows
all around
between the
One and many.

For a season
the greening leaves
of the trees
will hide the
decomposition of the dirt

until it is their time to
join the composting
and unification
of ALL.

Surely,
death must
preclude the ONE-ing
of ALL.

BEESWAX CANDLES AT VESPERS

A brokenness
in my body
at the end of the day
weakly calls to weakness
asking for a silent peace
to attend my way.

O God make speed
to save,
O LORD make haste
to help us.

Incense rises
on some altar
daises in the
islands of
Greece,
on the Holy Mountain,
and at Sinai.

I hear the crackle
of the candle flame, slowly
hissing as it burns
the beeswax up and
through the wick.

As wax melts from
the fire, may those
who hate THEE flee from
before Your throne.

Words rise up,
all over the world,
as day comes to rest
in the evening
vesperal light.

O Gladsome Light,
sing on from the
fourth century,
call our hearts
in the groan that is a
chant and a cry.

Now lettest
Thou Thy servant
depart in peace,
according
to THY word.

Take everything that
rises
and everything that
makes its way
in
and meld them into
one offering
which YOU eat
and regurgitate
for YOUR young.

Everything
that rises
must converge.

OWL MOON

I have tucked my fears
behind the silvery
glow of the evening moon.

She seems less
attached
to the things that
weigh me down;

to the things that
ask me to give
them attention
when I am already
living my life.

I will hide
my worries
under the pungent tuber
of the skunk cabbage.

She will never
even hear the
songs they sing in
my ear—they
are nothing to her.

From out of
the stillness and
silent reflection
of the lake

I will take my
strength.

She watches
it all go by
and only carries
the faintest
image of all
happenings
on her surface.

With the new
sun,
that image
is no longer
there.

SPRING PEEPERS

The earth has reached up
and swallowed the last
of the snow of winter.

Gone for two weeks.

A lull in life
became
dusty brown and
dried like
the leaves lying
all around on
the ground.

We waited.

Peepers slowly
began their song
on the southern lake;

a few the
first day,
but no more.

Our longing for
the full-echo sound
of peepers almost
shouting

all around our heads

brought them out;
slowly,
slowly,
gently.

And then it
happened.

Their song
has swelled
to full bloom
and I am
deafened by
their screaming chant
that takes me into my heart.

The sound of the peepers
has been from all time,

and they are back.

HISSING RAINDROPS

The ground -

it
is so dry -

you can almost
hear a hissing
as the drops
of rain

touch the face
of the earth.

The heat
comes up
off of the
surface

just about
dissolving
the rain

as it touches down.

Spattering
and hissing,
this rain

is long overdue.

Like the
opening of a flower
you have long
awaited

these drops
of moisture -

emancipating the
world from heat -

clearly open the
heart in a
ravenous hunger.

ALL IN THE TASTING

It is this taste -

this early morning
sweetness
and union
with the
One who
can make
the stars
just a bit more dim

than they were
yesterday -

the One who can
cause the
breeze to
cut a path
across
the surface of
the still, still waters
of the lake

it is the
taste of
this One
in my heart

that I have come
to long for.

VEIL

Without so much as a
breath or motion
I found out I am what I
was all this time
and did not know.

How is it for so long
we are not what we think?

How is it we
make all our days out
to be the veil
and not the great depth
beyond the fabric of
the gauze.

Let it tear.
Let it fall.
I am
what I have been
for all eternity.

I am that.
I am this.

I am.